D1270997

Elon Musk

Space Entrepreneur

By Ryan Nagelhout

LUCENT
P R E S S

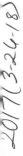

Published in 2017 by
Lucent Press, an Imprint of Greenhaven Publishing, LLC
353 3rd Avenue
Suite 255
New York, NY 10010

Designer: Deanna Paternostro
Editor: Katie Kawa

Cataloging-in-Publication Data

Names: Nagelhout, Ryan.
Title: Elon Musk: space entrepreneur / Ryan Nagelhout.
Description: New York : Lucent Press, 2017. | Series: People in the
news| Includes index.
Identifiers: ISBN 9781534560352 (library bound) | ISBN
9781534560369 (ebook)
Subjects: LCSH: Musk, Elon--Juvenile literature. | Businesspeople-
-United States--Biography--Juvenile literature. | Businesspeople--
South Africa--Biography--Juvenile literature.
Classification: HC102.5.M88 N34 2017 | DDC 332.1'78--dc23

Printed in the United States of America

CPSIA compliance information: Batch #CW17KL: For further information contact Greenhaven Publishing LLC,
New York, New York at 1-844-317-7404.

Please visit our website, www.greenhavenpublishing.com. For
a free color catalog of all our high-quality books, call toll free
1-844-317-7404 or fax 1-844-317-7405.

Contents

Foreword

We live in a world where the latest news is always available and where it seems we have unlimited access to the lives of the people in the news. Entire television networks are devoted to news about politics, sports, and entertainment. Social media has allowed people to have an unprecedented level of interaction with celebrities. We have more information at our fingertips than ever before. However, how much do we really know about the people we see on television news programs, social media feeds, and magazine covers?

Despite the constant stream of news, the full stories behind the lives of some of the world's most newsworthy men and women are often unknown. Who was Taylor Swift before she was a pop music phenomenon? What does LeBron James do when he is not playing basketball? What inspired Elon Musk to dream as big as he does?

This series aims to answer questions like these about some of the biggest names in pop culture, sports, politics, and technology. While the subjects of this series come from all walks of life and areas of expertise, they share a common magnetism that has made them all captivating figures in the public eye. They have shaped the world in some unique way, and—in many cases—they are poised to continue to shape the world for many years to come.

These biographies are not just a collection of basic facts. They tell compelling stories that show how each figure grew to become a powerful public personality. Each book aims to paint a complete, realistic picture of its subject—from the challenges they overcame to the controversies they caused. In doing so, each book reinforces the idea that even the most famous faces on the news are real people who are much more complex than we are often shown in brief video clips or sound bites. Readers are also reminded that there is even more to a person than what they present to the world through social media posts, press releases, and interviews. The whole story of a person's life can only be discovered by digging beneath the surface of their public persona, and that is what this series allows readers to do.

The books in this series are filled with enlightening quotes from speeches and interviews given by the subjects, as well as quotes and anecdotes from those who know their story best: family, friends, coaches, and colleagues. All quotes are noted to provide guidance for further research. Detailed lists of additional resources are also included, as are timelines, indexes, and unique photographs. These text features come together to enhance the reading experience and encourage readers to dive deeper into the stories of these influential men and women.

Fame can be fleeting, but the subjects featured in this series have real staying power. They have fundamentally impacted their respective fields and have achieved great success through hard work and true talent. They are men and women defined by their accomplishments, and they are often seen as role models for the next generation. They have left their mark on the world in a major way, and their stories are meant to inspire readers to leave their mark, too.

Introduction

Comic Book Comparisons

Comic book characters are not real. The characters you may read about in comics or see in movies based on them are just that—characters. Comic book writers try to make many of their characters something more than just human. They create beings capable of things not thought to be possible by an ordinary man or woman.

If there was one person worthy of comic book comparisons, however, Elon Musk is not a bad pick. Many have compared him to Tony Stark, the billionaire inventor and wearer of the suit that has created the famous superhero Iron Man. Musk himself has not become a superhero, but he has created a growing empire full of superhuman ambitions.

Musk hopes that cars—both affordable and luxury models—will become electric, driverless, and safer than any car controlled by a human being. Perhaps more interestingly, he wants humans to establish lasting legacies on places beyond Earth. Musk's SpaceX company has taken on the challenge of keeping the International Space Station (ISS) supplied and manned, and he is already looking farther into space. He wants to land humans on Mars and create a safe and secure compound on the Red Planet.

Musk's ambition—much like that of the fictional billionaire

Elon Musk's goals might seem like something out of a futuristic comic book, but he hopes to make them very real.

Stark—has exceeded the known capabilities of humans to this point in history—and yet he has shown the hope, drive, and vision to create something more.

"What Musk has developed that so many of the entrepreneurs in Silicon Valley lack is a meaningful worldview," wrote biographer Ashlee Vance in *Elon Musk: Tesla, SpaceX, and the Quest for a Fantastic Future*. Vance continued,

> *He's the possessed genius on the grandest quest anyone has ever concocted. He's less a CEO chasing riches than a general marshaling troops to secure victory. Where (Facebook founder) Mark Zuckerberg wants to help you share baby photos, Musk wants to ... well ... save the human race from self-imposed or accidental annihilation.[1]*

Like most superheroes from the pages of comic books, Musk wants to save people and create a better world, and he plans to do these things using technological advances that also seem to be straight out of the pages of fiction.

Working with Iron Man

Much like Tony Stark, Elon Musk has enjoyed his wealth and growing fame. Fast cars, big houses, and jets have become a staple of Musk's public persona. The fictional and real billionaires have actually crossed paths on the big screen, when Musk appeared in the film *Iron Man 2*, talking to Tony Stark about an electric jet. Musk also reportedly helped actor Robert Downey Jr. get into character before he began filming as Tony Stark. Meeting Musk helped the actor make his character feel more realistic, and it has been said that the film version of Tony Stark is basically a heightened version of Musk.

Jon Favreau, who directed *Iron Man* and *Iron Man 2*, said that Musk even let Marvel film part of the sequel at SpaceX.

It has been reported that Musk helped Robert Downey Jr., shown here in *Iron Man 2,* prepare for his role as Tony Stark.

"*Iron Man 2*, we filmed at SpaceX," Favreau told *Recode* in 2016. "He let us film there for free. He's been a very good friend of the Marvel family there, and we've maintained a friendship with him."[2]

Real Work Toward Real Change

In 2016, when Musk met with U.S. Secretary of Defense Ash Carter at the Pentagon in Washington, D.C., he joked about being the real Iron Man. Musk used the social networking website Twitter to send a link to an article that asked "What was Elon Musk doing at the Pentagon?" answering the question by saying, "Something about a flying metal suit…"[3] This is a reference to Iron Man's famous costume. He has clearly had fun with his role as Iron Man's influence, but the real reason for his visit was mostly likely a meeting about SpaceX being part of an $82.7 million deal to help the military launch an important satellite into orbit. Still, Musk and comic books are forever interlocked. His view on the world—especially in terms of what businesses should do for people—is still impacted today by the science fiction and superhero stories he read as a child.

"Maybe I read too many comics as a kid," Musk once said. "In the comics, it always seems like they were trying to save the world. It seemed like one should try to make the world a better place because the inverse makes no sense."[4]

The main difference between Musk and Stark is obvious: Musk is real. Although Musk's life may have inspired fiction, his plans for the future are anything but fictional. This billionaire wants to change the world in a way the writers of *Iron Man* can only write in movie scripts and comics. Musk's work—as lofty as it may seem—is real.

Chapter One

South Africa to Canada

Elon Reeve Musk was born in South Africa on June 28, 1971. He grew up in Pretoria, the administrative capital city of South Africa that is about an hour by car from the country's largest city, Johannesburg. Musk got his unusual name from his great-grandfather—John Elon Haldeman. Elon's maternal grandparents—Joshua and Wyn Haldeman—lived an exciting life together. They are believed to have been the first couple to fly from South Africa to Australia in a single-engine plane.

Elon's parents—Maye and Errol—are both very smart. Maye is a model and still appears in magazines, advertisements, and even music videos. She has also worked as a dietician for many years. Errol is a pilot, sailor, and engineer. Elon has two siblings. His younger brother Kimbal worked with him on early ventures and is a millionaire today. His sister Tosca is a film producer.

Elon's father knew at a young age that Elon was smart like him and his wife. However, Errol also came to see that his oldest son was very different and did not think the way other children did. "The kind of things he would come up with as a youngster was always surprising," Errol told a radio station in Johannesburg. "When he was very small, he would ask

Elon's mother, Maye, has remained close to Elon throughout his life. She continues to work as a model and has even appeared in one of Beyoncé's music videos.

me 'where is the whole world?' when he was three or four. It was these sorts of questions that made me realize that he was a little different."[5]

Lost in His Head

Early in his life, Elon's family thought he might be deaf. He would drift off into his own world at times, unable to focus on anything happening around him. Often, people would talk to him, and he would have a distant look in his eyes. He did not seem to know anyone else was there. His parents did not know if he could not hear them or if he was just lost within his own thoughts. Doctors ran tests on young Elon to see what was wrong. They also removed his adenoids. The adenoids are part of a child's lymphatic system and are located in the head near the nose and throat. Sometimes, these glands can become enlarged and limit hearing.

Elon was not having trouble hearing, however. He just preferred to be lost in his own thoughts. His mother has revealed that this trait has not gone away with age. "He goes into his brain, and then you see he is in another world," Maye Musk said. "He still does that. Now I just leave him be because I know he is designing a new rocket or something."[6]

Elon said that at age five or six, he learned how to block out everything else and focus on a single thing:

It seems as though the part of the brain that's usually reserved for visual processing—the part that is used to process images coming in from my eyes—gets taken over by internal thought processes … I can't do this as much now because there are so many things demanding my attention but, as a kid, it happened a lot. That large part of your brain that's used to handle incoming images gets used for internal thinking.[7]

In these moments, Elon could see things fully formed in his mind. He could imagine changing shapes and creating things that did not yet exist, but he could see them. This ability to visualize things that could be became very important as Elon grew into the visionary he is known as today.

A Tough Childhood

Though Elon's childhood was full of adventure and privilege, it was not easy. His parents divorced before he was 10 years old. Maye Musk moved to Durban, on the eastern coast of South Africa. After a couple of years living with his mother, Elon decided to live with his father. Kimbal soon joined him. Elon's mother could not understand why he moved in with his father, and Musk rarely talks about Errol today.

Errol Musk's home had many books, and he took his sons on exotic trips. However, Elon was not happy. He was a loner and did not have an easy time making friends. He was made fun of for his strange name and his tendency to stare off into space and think. To cope, Elon took to the things he loved—reading

Elon lived with Errol Musk, shown here, after his parent's divorce, but today, he seldom talks about his father to the press. His children are not allowed to meet their grandfather.

and learning.

"It would certainly be accurate to say that I did not have a good childhood," Musk once said. "It may sound good. It was not absent of good, but it was not a happy childhood. It was like misery."[8]

Musk bounced between a few different schools and did not make many friends. When he was attending Bryanston High School, he missed a week of school when some bullies pushed him down a flight of stairs. They then kicked and punched him for good measure, bloodying him enough that he went to the hospital. Later in life, he had plastic surgery to correct a problem with his nose that stemmed from the incident.

The bullies did not stop there. They even beat up and picked on people they thought were Elon's friends, which further isolated him.

Things at school were better for Elon when he began attending Pretoria Boys High School, a prestigious school filled with ambitious students. However, Elon did not like sports, which was considered unusual for a young man in South Africa, and he was not one of the top students in his class. He was bored by some subjects and did not worry about getting the best grades.

Still, Elon was a smart, quiet boy who loved science fiction and computers. He fantasized about exploring space and loved Douglas Adams's *The Hitchhiker's Guide to the Galaxy*. Always thinking big, even at a young age, Elon said that Adams's book taught him an important lesson about what he should do with his life:

[Adams] points out that one of the really tough things is figuring out what questions to ask. Once you figure out the question, then the answer is relatively easy. I came to the conclusion that really we should aspire to increasing the scope and scale of human consciousness in order to better understand what questions to ask. The only thing that makes sense to do is strive for greater collective enlightenment.[9]

"Good at Making Life Miserable"

Errol Musk is considered a sore spot for conversation among his children, particularly Elon. Maye also does not speak publicly about what happened during their marriage. However, there have been a few occasions when Elon Musk has spoken about his father, and the picture that emerged was one of a difficult and domineering man. He was a talented engineer whose home was a fun place for his sons to live, but he inflicted a kind of psychological trauma on his sons that they still do not speak readily about.

Elon once said of his father, "He's good at making life miserable—that's for sure. He can take any situation no matter how good it is and make it bad. He's not a happy man ... I don't know how someone becomes like he is." Maye echoed her son's sentiments and repeated the reason why neither she nor her children reveal too much about their time with Errol: "He is not nice to anyone. I don't want to tell stories because they are horrendous. You know, you just don't talk about it. There are kids and grandkids involved."[1]

1. Quoted in Ashlee Vance, *Elon Musk: Tesla, SpaceX, and the Quest for a Fantastic Future*. New York, NY: HarperCollins, 2015, p. 37.

This was a lofty goal for a teenager, but Elon's outlook on life was shaped by the books he read as a child. He read a lot—up to 10 hours a day. By the age of eight, he had run out of books to read at the library. He read the entire *Encyclopaedia Britannica* cover to cover and memorized its contents. Elon was a bit of a know-it-all, shouting out answers before questions were finished, and he could spout information off the top of his head without having to look it up. Elon had a photographic memory and loved to learn. He was the perfect kind of child to embrace the coming technological and informational revolution brought on by computers.

Finding Computers and Blastar

Elon saw a computer for the first time when he was around 10 years old. He begged for one for himself, saved up his own money, and soon owned a Commodore VIC-20. He threw himself into learning everything about computers. Elon taught himself how to code, or build computer programs. He absorbed guides to programming and quickly learned skills other programmers needed months to learn.

Elon also became interested in rockets. Because none of the more popular rocket-making kits were made in South Africa, Elon would often make his own rockets—and rocket explosives—for himself, his brother, and his cousins Russ,

Peter and Lyndon Rive are cousins of the Musks who later went into business with Elon.

Lyndon, and Peter Rive. Elon would mix chemicals and put them inside canisters; then, he would blast these rockets into the sky. The chemicals were, of course, incredibly dangerous. When speaking about his childhood experiments with rockets, Elon said,

It is remarkable how many things you can get to explode ... Saltpeter, sulfur, and charcoal are the basic ingredients for gunpowder, and then if you combine a strong acid with a strong alkaline, that will generally release a lot of energy. Granulated chlorine with brake fluid—that's quite impressive. I'm lucky I have all my fingers.[10]

Even at a very early age, Elon was fascinated by space. When Elon taught himself to code, he soon found himself making his own video games. In 1984, Elon shared the code he wrote for *Blastar*, a space-based video game he coded when he was 12. He sold the 167 lines of code for *Blastar* to the South African trade magazine *PC and Office Technology* for $500. The code for *Blastar* appeared in the December 1984 edition of the magazine, with this description: "In this game you have to destroy an alien space freighter, which is carrying deadly Hydrogen Bombs and Status Beam Machines. This game makes good use of sprites and animation, and in this sense makes the listing worth reading."[11]

In 2015, a software engineer at Google—Tomas Lloret Llinares—took the code from the magazine and redesigned it to work online. It can still be played on the Internet for free today.

"*Blastar* is mostly a mix of *Space Invaders* and *Asteroid*, though it's much more basic," Sean O'Kane wrote in 2015 for the news website *The Verge*. "There is never more than two ships on the screen, there are few sound effects, and—like many games of its time—it really has no ending. It's almost unimpressive; that is, until you remember that it was made by a 12-year-old in 1984."[12]

Elon's love of video games also led to an early business venture. He, Kimbal, and their cousins tried to start an arcade when they were still under 18 years old. They found a spot to open it, got a lease for the building, and even started the process to get

Kimbal Musk, shown here, went into business with Elon at an early age, selling things around the neighborhood and even attempting to open an arcade with Elon and their cousins before they turned 18.

a business permit before they realized someone over the age of 18 needed to sign paperwork for them. Errol Musk would not let them start the arcade, but the cousins would later go into business together on a much larger scale.

Switching Continents

Elon did not want to stay in South Africa forever. After high school, he attended the University of Pretoria, studying physics and engineering. However, he was not focused on his studies, and he dropped out after five months. Elon's true dream was to go to America. To achieve this, he first started in Canada. Elon gained Canadian citizenship through his mother, who was a Canadian citizen, and moved to Canada when he was 17.

Elon landed in North America in June 1988, found a pay phone, and tried to call his great-uncle, who he was supposed to stay with upon arriving in Montreal, Quebec. However, his great-uncle had moved to Minnesota, meaning Elon had nowhere to stay. He spent a few days in Montreal at a hostel before he traveled across Canada looking for relatives to stay with. His mother had family in various parts of the country, so Elon traveled to Swift Current, a town in southwest Saskatchewan with a population of 15,000 people.

For the next year of his life, Elon worked a number of different odd jobs. He worked in another tiny town in Saskatchewan called Waldeck when he turned 18, shoveling out grain bins and growing vegetables on his cousin's farm. He also used a chainsaw to cut logs in Vancouver, British Columbia.

Elon even made $18 an hour doing a dangerous job—cleaning out the boiler room of a lumber mill. He described the hazardous work in Vance's biography:

You have to put on this hazmat suit and then shimmy through this little tunnel that you can barely fit in … Then, you have a shovel and you take the sand and goop and other residue, which

Against Apartheid

One of the reasons Elon left South Africa was to avoid mandatory service in the military. South African white males over the age of 16 were required to serve in the nation's armed forces. This was part of apartheid, or "apartness," which was the systemized discrimination against people of color in South Africa that existed for decades. Nonwhite citizens were never drafted in the military during apartheid, which ended in South Africa in 1994.

"I don't have an issue with serving in the military per se, but serving in the South African army suppressing black people just didn't seem like a really good way to spend time,"[1] Elon once said.

That compulsory military service was finally ended in 1993, but by then, Elon had long left the country; he was in America studying business and physics.

1. Quoted in Biography.com editors, "Elon Musk Biography," Biography.com, November 21, 2016. www.biography.com/people/elon-musk-20837159#hyperloop.

is still steaming hot, and you have to shovel it through the same hole you came through. There is no escape. Someone else on the other side has to shovel it into a wheelbarrow. If you stay in there for more than 30 minutes you get too hot and die.[13]

While Elon worked and explored Canada, his mother and siblings were also in the process of moving there. They joined Elon in Canada, and Elon was happy to be surrounded by his immediate family again. In 1989, Elon began studying at Queen's University in Kingston, Ontario. There, he would build and sell computers and computer parts to earn extra money. He and Kimbal also cold-called interesting people they read about in the newspaper. On one occasion, they even

At the University of Pennsylvania, which is sometimes called Penn, Elon Musk demonstrated a knack for applying scientific concepts to business plans. This talent helped make him a successful entrepreneur.

had lunch with an executive at the Bank of Nova Scotia, who later offered Elon an internship there. The internship would be an important step in some of Musk's later ambitions with online banking.

Elon excelled in college. He found people that did not make

fun of him for his intellect, and he studied the things that interested him. He made friends and found a place where his ambition could not only be appreciated, but nurtured. In 1992, he achieved his dream of living in the United States when he transferred to a school there. The University of Pennsylvania offered him a scholarship, and he moved there to get an economics degree from the Wharton School of Business. He also earned a bachelor's degree in physics. Elon continued to thrive in college, writing well-received papers about the future potential of solar energy and other business ideas.

Even before Elon had finished school, he was ready to explore the western coast of the United States. In the summer of 1994, he and his brother bought an old BMW 320i. They packed up and drove across the country, their focus set on California. It was time for the Musks to get to work.

Chapter Two

Start-Ups and Sales

Elon Musk's arrival in California was not initially for business, but for school. Musk also had two internships while he was still at Penn. The first was in Los Gatos, at a company called Pinnacle Research Institute. There, he studied ultracapacitors and how they could be used in electric vehicles and possibly in weapons. His other internship was at Rocket Science Games, a Palo Alto video game start-up. There, he was coding for a company that wanted to move video games to compact discs (CDs) to improve the quality of their graphics and increase the amount of information they could hold.

Peter Barrett, an engineer who helped start Rocket Science Games, described the work Musk did during his internship: "We brought him in to write some very menial low-level code … He was completely unflappable. After a short while, I don't think anyone was giving him direction, and he ended up making what he wanted to make."[14]

For two summers in a row, Musk traveled to California. Then, he went out there for good after graduation. At first, he was going to pursue a doctorate in physics at Stanford University. He lasted two days at Stanford before dropping out and focusing all his energy on capitalizing on the dot-com boom, or the rise in investments in Internet-based companies. Elon convinced his brother Kimbal to move out west with him, and the two started to brainstorm ideas for Internet businesses.

Zip2

In 1995, Elon and Kimbal created Global Link Information Network, a start-up that eventually became known as Zip2. The idea came from a salesperson who wanted to set up an online version of listings that could be sold with the physical Yellow

Elon Musk's interests in science and technology have made him a popular speaker at conferences and with the media. However, when Zip2 was first starting, Kimbal did most of the talking to potential clients and investors about the company, while Elon did the coding.

Pages, which list business addresses and other information about local companies.

Musk liked the idea, but he thought the salesperson had no idea how the Internet actually worked. "Elon said, 'These guys don't know what they're talking about. Maybe this is something we can do,'"[15] Kimbal recalled. Zip2 was an attempt to convince restaurants, stores, barbershops, and other small businesses that they should have a presence online. In 1995, this was a fairly revolutionary concept. Most businesses did not have websites at the time and did not understand how the Internet could help customers find them. Musk's idea was simple: make a database of businesses, make it searchable, and have a map that could show people how close they are to each kind of business and how to get to the place they wanted to go.

The Musks borrowed $28,000 from their father, Errol, to start Global Link Information Network. Musk coded the entire project himself in a tiny office space in Palo Alto. He used a map database called Navteq, which allowed him to use their technology for free, and he collected information about local businesses. These two groups of data were then put into a database that allowed them to be used together.

"I wrote something that allowed you to keep maps and directions on the Internet and then something that allowed you to do online manipulation of content—kind of a really advanced blogging system," Musk said during a presentation at Stanford University in October 2003. "Then we started talking to small newspapers and media companies and so forth. We started getting some interest."[16]

The start-up was originally run by just six people—the Musks, three sales people they hired through a newspaper ad, and Greg Kouri. He was a friend of Maye Musk who moved to California in 1996 to help establish Zip2 after initially giving Musk $6,000 to help with the initial costs.

Pitching the power of the Internet in the mid-1990s—before it became the everyday necessity it is today—was tough with such a small staff, but the team made some headway into businesses over time. "I mean, half of the time it'd be like 'What's the internet?' Even in Silicon Valley," Musk said. "But eventually somebody would buy it and we get a little bit of money from them."[17]

The tiny office also doubled as an apartment for Musk in the early months of Zip2. He slept in the office and showered at a nearby YMCA. Eventually, Elon and Kimbal rented out a small apartment, but Elon still seemed to live at the office; employees would find him asleep at his desk when they came in for work the next morning.

Although Musk is a billionaire now, he was not always working from a place of financial stability. The early days of Zip2 were especially difficult financially. "Things were pretty tough in the early going. I didn't have any money," Musk said. "In fact, I had negative money. I had huge student debts."[18]

The start-up got its Internet access from an Internet Service Provider (ISP) that was one floor down from its office. Musk actually drilled a hole in the office wall himself to run a cable to the ISP. This helped the company keep costs down while Musk and his team grew their business and looked for venture capitalists (VCs) to invest money in the company.

"We … had a really tiny revenue stream," Musk said. "But we actually had more revenue than we had expenses, so when we went and talked to VCs we could actually say we had positive cash flow."[19]

VC Money

In 1996, Mohn Davidow Ventures invested $3 million into Global Link Information Network, which then officially changed its name to Zip2. Musk became Zip2's chief technology officer, and Rich Sorkin was hired as the company's chief executive officer (CEO). The cash infusion also meant Elon and Kimbal could finally get rid of their BMW, which broke down all the time. One time, an intern borrowed the car and

Zip2's newspaper clients included the *New York Times*.

a wheel fell off. The two brothers were given money to buy new cars. Kimbal bought a BMW 3 Series, while Elon bought a Jaguar E-Type.

That car represented a kind of dream come true for Musk. He told *Forbes* magazine's Hannah Elliott, "When I was 17 or so, I was given a book of classic convertibles, and I looked through them all and the one I liked the best was the E-Type Jaguar. I said, 'Well if I can ever afford it, that's the one I'm going to get.' So that's the one I bought."[20]

Musk was proud of his first real car, but it was not much more reliable than his first, wheel-less one. "It kept breaking down on me and causing me all sorts of trouble,"[21] Musk said.

Not only did the investment allow for fancy new cars for the Musk brothers, the company began to shift its focus away from adding small businesses to its database and toward selling software to larger companies that needed help setting up their own databases and web services. Many of these companies were newspapers. Zip2 trademarked the slogan "We Power the Press" and started working with media companies such as the *New York Times*, which paired with Zip2 to make a local directory website called New York Today. Other newspapers such as the *Chicago Tribune* and news companies such as Knight Ridder and Hearst also worked with Zip2 to get online, trying to compete with free classifieds websites such as Craigslist.

As the company got larger, Musk had to loosen his control over many different aspects of it. New coders were hired who rewrote much of his code. This bothered Musk, but in the end, many of them were more talented and polished as coders. Musk, who taught himself how to code, was not as efficient as many of the new faces. His code often contained what developers call "hairballs." These were large chunks of code that were difficult to work with and often caused major problems coders could not trace. Hairballs are often a problem with self-taught coders, but Musk still preferred his own work to that of others. He would sometimes change lines of code after other coders had left, and he turned other engineers and employees against him because he could be quite harsh in his criticism of their work.

Musk struggled to accept the changes at Zip2 and often battled with others in the company who wanted to take control of various aspects of the day-to-day operation. In addition, his management style at Zip2 often bothered his coworkers. He would set very optimistic deadlines for projects and then push his employees to meet what were often impossible demands. "If you asked Elon how long it would take to do something, there was never anything in his mind that would take more than an hour," Jim Ambras, who was the vice president of engineering at Zip2, once said. "We came to interpret an hour as really taking a day or two and if Elon ever did say something would take a day, we allowed for a week or two weeks."[22]

Struggles with CitySearch

By 1997, Zip2 had moved to a nicer building for its offices. However, the company was not the only major force in its market anymore. Soon, other database companies were growing their own customer base and expanding their services. A company called CitySearch quickly became a rival of Zip2. However, instead of battling one another, the two companies announced a merger, or a joining of their companies. This deal was worth an estimated $300 million.

"This is a true merger of equals," Musk told the website ZDNet in 1998 when the merger was announced. "This isn't a merger motivated by rationalization or something else. The reason for this merger is category leadership and meeting demand that we see in the market ... We found that being No. 1 in the category seems to matter more than being numbers 2 or 3."[23]

However, the merger was difficult. The companies did not see eye to eye on their finances and which employees would leave the merged company once the deal went through. Musk, who at first was in favor of the merger, turned against it. There was a power struggle on both sides of the merger, and eventually, it fell apart. CitySearch and Zip2 ended their merger plans in May 1998. CitySearch then merged with Ticketmaster Online in August of that same year.

With their merger plans now dead, Zip2 needed to figure out what came next. The company was losing money, and its leaders were unsure what direction the company should head: directly to the consumer or to businesses, which they would help from behind the scenes.

Some suggested to Musk that he should sell the company and look to work on his next big idea. "There was a lot of backlash and finger-pointing," said Derek Proudian, a VC with Mohr Davidow, the group that initially invested in Zip2. "Elon wanted to be CEO, but I said 'This is your first company. Let's find an acquirer and make some money, so you can do your second, third, and fourth company.'"[24]

Selling It Off

In February 1999, the computer company Compaq offered $307 million for Zip2. It wanted to boost its own Altavista search engine with Zip2's local listings and technology. Mohr Davidow made $60 million on the deal, while Elon made $22 million and Kimbal made $15 million. At the time, it was the largest cash-only purchase of an Internet company. The payout, though, did come at a price—both Elon and Kimbal left Zip2 for good. Elon was already thinking about the future, and he wanted to start a

Musk's boyish looks have made many underestimate him throughout his life, but the growth and sale of Zip2 proved he was a budding Silicon Valley star.

The McLaren F1

Elon Musk celebrated a bit after leaving Zip2. In 1999, he bought one of the most luxurious cars in the world— a McLaren F1. The car, which costs $800,000 brand new, has gone for even larger amounts of money at auction. Musk's McLaren was delivered from a dealer in Florida, and it was apparently desired by more moguls than just Musk, including fashion designer Ralph Lauren. The delivery of Musk's silver McLaren was even filmed for part of a documentary about millionaires.

"Three years ago, I was showering at the YMCA and sleeping on the office floor," Musk told an interviewer. "Now I have a million-dollar car and a quite a few creature comforts." Musk also bragged about the car's rarity: "There's 62 McLaren F1s in the world," he said. "And I will own one of them."[1]

Musk actually drove the McLaren daily, putting 11,000 miles (17,703 km) on the car before he crashed it into an embankment one day while showing the car off to his colleague, Peter Thiel. Musk, of course, moved on

company at which he could be CEO.

Still, despite its issues, Musk said he learned a lot about how to run a company at Zip2:

I had never really run a team of any sort before … I'd never been a sports captain or a captain of anything or managed a single person. I had to think, Okay, what are the things that affect how a team functions. The first obvious assumption would be that other people will behave like you. But that's not true. Even if they would like to behave like you, they don't necessarily have all the assumptions or information that you have in your mind. So, if I

to other cars—including ones he designed himself—but the McLaren F1 was always a benchmark he used when it came to automotive excellence.

1. Quoted in Benjamin Zhang, "Watch a Young Elon Musk Take Delivery of His McLaren F1 Hypercar—Before He Wrecked It," *Business Insider*, June 8. 2015. www.businessinsider.com/elon-musk-mclaren-f1-hypercar-wrecked-it-2015-6.

Musk was one of the few people in the world to own a McLaren F1. A 1996 model of the car is shown here.

know a certain set of things, and I talk to a replica of myself but only communicate half the information, you can't expect that the replica would come to the same conclusion. You have to put yourself in a position where you say, 'Well, how would this sound to them, knowing what they know?'[25]

Out of Zip2, Musk took a few years of experience dealing with employees and venture capitalists, aspirations for something bigger, and more than $20 million. He was ready to start his second company.

Chapter **Three**

X Marks the Money

Elon Musk, a newly-minted multimillionaire, did not sit on his money. Instead, he invested most of his money into his next business venture. He moved into a larger condo and renovated it, and he bought his McLaren and a small plane. After those expenses, about $12 million of his own money went into his new start-up.

Musk once likened his plans for spending and investing his money to a poker game:

> I could go and buy one of the islands in the Bahamas and turn it into my personal fiefdom, but I am much more interested in trying to ... create a new company ... It's sort of like a series of poker games, and now I've gone on to a more high-stakes poker game and just carried those chips with me ... I haven't ... taken my winnings and spent a good chunk of it; I've really put almost all of it back into the new game.[26]

Instead of spending his new millions, Musk turned to banking. His time as an intern at the Bank of Nova Scotia taught him many things about how the banking world works. Musk came to believe that banking was a large business that was not

Musk threw a large amount of the fortune he made at Zip2
into his new venture, which was a big risk many entrepreneurs
would not take for fear of failure.

adaptable to change. He thought he could use the Internet to create an online bank that would be better served for the future, which he believed would continue to be digital.

Musk thought back to his time in Nova Scotia and believed something could be done to break banks out of following one another's lead. He thought an online bank could change the way things were done in the industry. He remembered a specific instance where the Bank of Nova Scotia would not follow through on what he thought was a "no-brainer" investment in South America because the company had lost money investing in the region in the past:

> Later in life, as I competed against the banks, I would think back to this moment, and it gave me confidence. All the bankers did was copy what everyone else did. If everyone else ran off a ... cliff, they'd run right off a cliff with them. If there was a giant pile of gold sitting in the middle of the room and nobody was picking it up, they wouldn't pick it up, either.[27]

Starting X.com

Musk had talked about starting an Internet bank as far back as 1995 while he interned with Pinnacle Research, but he knew little about how the banking industry actually worked. Still, he realized that using the Internet was the perfect way to make a big change in the industry with a small investment. During his speech at Stanford University in 2003, Musk said, "You don't need some sort of big infrastructure improvement to do things with [money]. It's really just an entry in a database."[28]

Musk's initial plan was to create a fully-functional bank based online. He imagined a full-service bank with checking accounts, savings accounts, and financial investment services, as well as insurance options.

Going through the legal process of creating a real bank

was daunting, but Musk started work on his new plan even before Zip2 was sold. He openly courted engineers and other people in Zip2 about potentially joining a new venture. In March 1999, just a month after Zip2 was sold, he incorporated X.com, which was what he called his online banking company. Musk was its biggest shareholder. The company started in a house in Silicon Valley and later moved into an office in Palo Alto. There were some early issues with a cofounder that left Musk without many of his early hires when they abruptly left, but Musk knew starting a banking revolution was never going to be easy.

Eventually, X.com got a banking license and developed a partnership with the bank Barclays. X.com went live for public use on the night before Thanksgiving in 1999. An X.com employee said that Musk stayed in the office 48 straight hours after the website went live to make sure everything was working properly. Musk's hard work and vision seemed once again to be paying off; more than 200,000 people signed up for X.com in the first few months of its existence.

Another Merger

Musk's X.com was not the only Internet bank on the block, though. In fact, X.com was actually renting space to a group of people trying to do something very similar. Entrepreneurs Peter Thiel and Max Levchin had their own banking ideas. That start-up, Confinity, was originally created to develop a way to send money between small personal digital assistants called PalmPilots. It became a rival of X.com, even though it briefly operated out of the same building in Silicon Valley.

Confinity soon abandoned its initial plan and began working on an Internet-based and email-based payment service called PayPal. Both Confinity and X.com spent millions on advertising their services and giving people incentives to start banking online with their company. Musk pushed his employees to work quickly, and he worked more than

Peter Thiel, shown here, was a cofounder of Confinity, a company that later merged with X.com and became PayPal.

20 hours a day.

Soon, however, X.com and PayPal realized they needed to merge to survive. PayPal was popular, but the company was giving out $100,000 a day in rewards to customers joining the service. X.com had plenty of money on hand, but PayPal was running out. The new company they formed through the merger was still called X.com initially, and Musk remained its largest shareholder.

PayPal

Although the merger went through, combining the two companies was a messy process. The culture at PayPal was different than at X.com or Musk's Zip2. Thiel's company, though doing very similar things, operated differently and more loosely than Musk's venture.

In a 2007 story in *Fortune* magazine, Musk's strained relationship with Thiel and negative opinion of his managerial philosophy was evident: "Peter, Max, and I are not directly aligned philosophically. Peter's philosophy is pretty odd. It's not normal. He's a contrarian from an investing standpoint and thinks a lot about the singularity. I'm much less excited about that. I'm pro-human."[29]

Musk faced threats to his leadership even before the merger. When X.com was working toward its IPO—an initial public offering that allowed the company to be publicly traded on the stock market—Musk was initially pushed out as its CEO. Some in the company wanted more experienced leadership. Former Intuit head Bill Harris took over as CEO, but his time at the head of the company did not last very long.

When Musk became CEO again after Harris resigned, he wanted to change the way the company's technology worked. Musk wanted to use a Microsoft-based system instead of a Unix or Linux system. Many people inside the company threw a fit. Levchin and Thiel were strong advocates of Unix. What has been described as a kind of "holy war" broke out inside the company over these competing platforms, and the company's board replaced Musk as CEO with Thiel while Musk was on vacation in Australia. "That's the problem with vacations,"[30] Musk joked to *Fortune* in 2007.

Musk tried to fight the board's decision at first, and he was supported by some of his X.com employees. The unceremonious way Musk was replaced marked the start of many X.com employees leaving PayPal, which is what Thiel rebranded the company as after he took over as CEO. Though it was billed in the press as Musk resigning from the company he still held

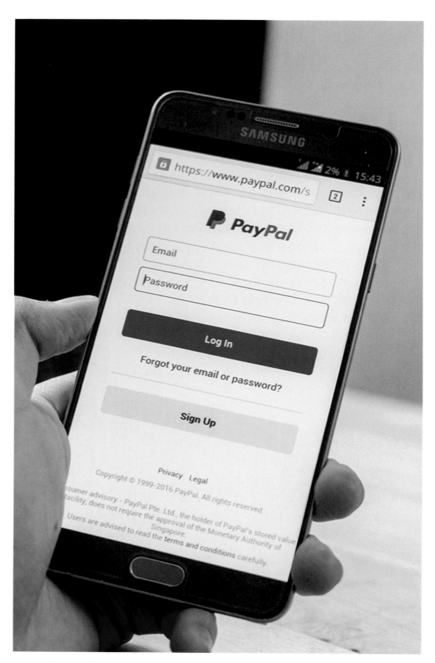

PayPal is still used by people doing business on the
Internet today.

the largest stake in, Musk was anything but happy about the move. However, he tried not to openly voice his frustrations in interviews at the time.

"One has to recognize where one's strengths lie," Musk told the website CNET in January 2002. "It's more interesting for me in the early stages of running a company, where the concentration is all on developing the product … I'm not really interested in administration."[31]

When Musk announced his departure from X.com, he said he planned to take a few months off once a new CEO was found before starting a new company. "I guess you can say that I'm a serial entrepreneur,"[32] he said.

Before his next venture, though, he had to cash out of X.com. Despite being ousted as the CEO, Musk stayed on as an advisor to the company and actually increased his stake in the business. The opportunity to cash out would come from eBay, which had been looking to strike up a deal with PayPal.

Cashing Out

PayPal made about $240 million in revenue per year by the end of 2001, and eBay had approached it about a potential acquisition. Millions of customers who were buying and selling goods on the online auction website used PayPal to securely exchange money, and the website wanted to take over those transactions. Musk was among those who pushed for PayPal to hold out for a bigger offer from eBay, which came in July of 2002 when eBay offered to pay $1.5 billion for the entire company. The board agreed with the terms, and Musk made $250 million on the transaction.

PayPal was another huge financial success for Musk, but it did not come without consequences. He developed a reputation for having a controversial management style. He had made enemies, and though plenty of people made huge financial gains from the company, relationships between the founders—sometimes referred to as "the PayPal Mafia"—were tense for years to come.

Later, these former coworkers would invest in each other's businesses and speak well of one another. However, Musk first had to speak out in the press about a book published about the company that "painted Musk as an egomaniacal, stubborn jerk, making wrong decisions at every turn."[33] Musk's response was a 2,200-word email to a gossip website known as Valleywag that was published as a rebuttal to previous remarks made about him on the site. Musk has used the press to his advantage over his career, but moves such as this one only drew more attention—and criticism—to his businesses and his management style.

Was Musk ready to be the CEO of his own company, or was he not CEO material, as some who worked with him suggested? Either way, with PayPal behind him, it was time for Musk's next bold venture—into space.

Elon and Justine

When Elon found out he had been removed from X.com as its CEO, he had been on a trip with his wife Justine. Elon met Justine—then Justine Wilson—in college when they were both attending Queen's University in Ontario. He spotted her from across a common room at school and decided he needed to meet her. Though she was a year younger than Elon, he immediately pursued a relationship with her. Elon pretended to bump into her on the steps of her dorm. He then asked her on a date to get ice cream, and she said yes. When Justine left a note on her door telling Elon she could not meet him, he did some research. He asked her friends where she studied and what her favorite kind of ice cream was.

"Several hours later," Justine wrote, "my head bent over my Spanish text in an overheated room in the student center, I heard a polite cough behind me. Elon was smiling awkwardly, two chocolate-chip ice cream cones dripping down his hands. He's not a man who takes no for an answer."[34]

Justine wanted to be a writer and was not looking for

Justine Musk is shown here in 2014 with Matt Petersen, who is an environmental activist and the chief sustainability officer for Los Angeles, California.

someone like Elon. She described wanting to be with a leather-jacket-wearing, mysterious person who would sweep her off her feet, which was certainly not Elon. However, he was very persistent, calling her often and sending her flowers. They were an on-again, off-again couple while Elon attended Penn, but Musk still sent her roses. They sometimes met in New York City for weekend visits, and when Musk moved to Silicon Valley, Justine visited more often. The two were married in January 2000.

Two months before that wedding, Musk asked Justine to sign an agreement about their finances. She then signed a financial and legal agreement called a postnup after their marriage. Musk's companies grew, and he became wealthy. Justine had time to work on her writing as Elon tended to his start-ups.

Their first child—Nevada Alexander—was born in 2000, but he died at 10 weeks old—just as PayPal's deal with eBay had been announced. Nevada had died of sudden infant death syndrome, which is commonly known as SIDS. Justine wrote about the incident in an article for *Marie Claire* magazine: "By the time the paramedics resuscitated him, he had been deprived of oxygen for so long that he was brain-dead. He spent three days on life support in a hospital in Orange County before we made the decision to take him off it. I held him in my arms when he died."[35]

Musk coped with Nevada's death by throwing himself into his work. "It made me extremely sad to talk about it," Musk said. "I'm not sure why I'd want to talk about extremely sad events. It does no good for the future. If you've got other kids and obligations, then wallowing in sadness does no good for anyone around you. I'm not sure what should be done in such situations."[36]

Justine, on the other hand, was open with her emotions after losing their son, which caused conflict in their marriage. Neither partner understood why the other was working through their grief in a way they found unacceptable. Instead of dealing with those issues, they threw themselves into trying to have more children. In 2004, twin boys—Griffin and Xavier—were born to the couple. The Musks also had triplets in 2006—Damian, Saxon, and Kai.

Emotionally, their marriage was difficult. Despite living

a "dream lifestyle," as Justine once called it, Elon worked constantly, and their relationship was strained. Justine raised their five children with a staff of household employees, but Elon's distance and strong personality—an alpha male demeanor typical in South African culture—began to wear on the marriage. Justine wrote about the end of their relationship in *Marie Claire*:

> *I told Elon, in a soft voice that was nonetheless filled with conviction, that I needed our life to change. I didn't want to be a sideline player in the multimillion-dollar spectacle of my husband's life. I wanted equality. I wanted partnership. I wanted to love and be loved, the way we had before he made all his millions.*

> *Elon agreed to enter counseling, but he was running two companies and carrying a planet of stress. One month and three sessions later, he gave me an ultimatum: Either we fix this marriage today or I will divorce you tomorrow, by which I understood he meant, Our status quo works for me, so it should work for you. He filed for divorce the next morning. I felt numb, but strangely relieved.*[37]

Elon and Justine were divorced in 2008. The postnuptial agreement Justine signed became a major factor in the messy legal proceedings that followed.

Trying Again

Shortly after Elon filed for divorce, he met actress Talulah Riley. The two married in 2010. Many, including Justine Musk, speculated that the divorce happened—at least in part—because of Riley. A *New York Times* article even suggested that Musk "ran off with an actress."[38] That article, among other things published in the media, including Justine's online blog posts about their divorce, prompted Elon to write an article for *Business Insider* in

A "Trophy Wife"

Writing for *Marie Claire* magazine, Justine Musk candidly described her marriage, which she felt turned her into something she never expected to be—a trophy wife:

It was a dream lifestyle, privileged and surreal. But the whirlwind of glitter couldn't disguise a growing void at the core. Elon was obsessed with his work: When he was home, his mind was elsewhere. I longed for deep and heartfelt conversations, for intimacy and empathy. And while I sacrificed a normal family life for his career, Elon started to say that I "read too much," shrugging off my book deadlines. This felt like a dismissal, and a stark reversal from the days when he was so supportive. When we argued—over the house or the kids' sleeping schedule—my faults and flaws came under the microscope. I felt insignificant in his eyes, and I began thinking about what effect our dynamic would have on our five young sons ...

which he attempted to respond to allegations against him and correct the public record:

Since I was accused of absconding with an actress in one of the biggest newspapers in the world, and moreover was quoted frequently in the article, this was assumed by many to be true. Let me be absolutely clear: it is not. I filed for divorce from Justine (for reasons I should not have to justify or make public) before I met Talulah Riley, the woman who is now my fiancé. The fact of the matter is that Talulah and I lived on opposite sides of the world and hadn't even known of each other's existence before the marriage with Justine ended.[39]

Justine and Musk split custody of their five boys and have

1. Justine Musk, "I Was a Starter Wife': Inside America's Messiest Divorce," *Marie Claire*, September 10, 2010. www.marieclaire.com/sex-love/advice/a5380/millionaire-starter-wife/.

eventually become cordial. They both agree on some things—especially that Musk's father, Errol, should never meet their children. Later on, Justine even became friends with Talulah during her marriage to Elon.

That marriage, too, had its own struggles. Musk became increasingly busy with his companies, and Riley spent time away from Musk pursuing her acting career. Two years after their marriage, Musk filed for divorce.

That divorce, however, did not last. They were remarried eighteen months later and spent the next two-and-a-half years together before filing for divorce again in early 2015. The two stressed that their second divorce was a mutual decision.

Even their second divorce, however, did not last. Musk withdrew the divorce petition in August 2015. They continued to spend time apart, though, and in 2016, Musk and Riley

Musk and actress Talulah Riley have had an on-again, off-again
relationship for many years.

filed for divorce—officially for a second time.

Riley teased the press by saying there was a chance she could get back together with Musk again: "When you've been with someone for eight years on and off, you really learn how to love them. He and I are very good at loving each other."[40]

Rumors about Musk's love life continue to fill websites and newspapers, but he does not have much time for romance between all the travel he does for business and the time he spends with his five sons:

I think the time allocated to the business and the kids is going fine … I would like to allocate more time to dating, though. I need to find a girlfriend. That's why I need to carve out just a little more time. I think maybe even another five to ten—how much time does a woman want a week? Maybe ten hours? That's kind of the minimum? I don't know.[41]

Chapter **Four**

Rockets to the Stars

Elon Musk's personal life has always seemed to take a backseat to his entrepreneurial ambitions. The Musks had moved to Los Angeles by the time PayPal was sold in 2002. There, Elon had begun to throw himself into a new industry: aeronautics. Southern California was a location of major importance to the space industry, with gigantic corporations such as Lockheed Martin calling Los Angeles home. Once in Los Angeles, Musk began thinking about Mars. More specifically, he began thinking about putting people on Mars.

Even before Musk was done with PayPal, he was thinking about space. Kevin Hartz, an early PayPal investor, recalled Musk talking about space travel while a group of PayPal founders were celebrating the company's success with a trip to Las Vegas before the company was bought by eBay: "We're all hanging out in this cabana at the Hard Rock Cafe, and Elon is there reading some obscure Soviet rocket manual that was all moldy and looked like it had been bought on eBay … He was studying it and talking openly about space travel and changing the world."[42]

Musk was shocked to find out that the National Aeronautics and Space Administration (NASA) had no definitive plans to explore Mars on its website. He described his reaction upon making this discovery in *Wired* magazine: "At first I thought, jeez, maybe I'm just looking in the wrong place ... Why was there no plan, no schedule? There was nothing. It seemed crazy."[43]

Musk donated $5,000 to the Mars Society, a group that wanted to explore and later settle the fourth planet from the sun. Though an amateur space explorer, Musk's interest turned some heads among people in the space industry. Robert Zubrin, the head of the Mars Society at the time, was particularly impressed: "He was much more interesting than some of the other millionaires ... He didn't know a lot about space, but he had a scientific mind. He wanted to know exactly what was being planned in regards to Mars and what the significance would be."[44]

Musk joined the Mars Society's board of directors and later became its director. He then moved on to found the Life to Mars Foundation. Musk's goal was to do a stunt that would turn heads. His most famous plan was to build a rocket out of old intercontinental ballistic missiles (ICBMs) to send mice to Mars. Musk thought a stunt like that would be costly, but it could rekindle discussions about the Red Planet among Americans, who had seemingly lost interest in space exploration.

A team of people worked with Musk to get a plan together to reach Mars. He even explored buying ICBMs from the Russians, taking trips to the country to negotiate. However, the plan fell through, as Musk decided the Russians were not taking him seriously and thought they were just trying to get as much money out of him as possible.

The Creation of SpaceX

Instead of working with the Russians, Musk thought he could design and build a proper rocket himself. For months, Musk studied physics, the aerospace industry, and how to build rockets.

"Thrillionaires"

Musk is the most successful "thrillionaire," a term coined for millionaire or billionaire tech moguls who have invested some of their fortune into "thrilling" endeavors, including the creation of spacecraft and rockets. Musk's SpaceX company is producing rockets for space travel and completing important missions that keep the ISS working properly. Others, such as Microsoft's cofounder Paul Allen and the Virgin Group's Richard Branson, compete in rocket competitions and are looking to create similar companies with the goal of privatizing spaceflight. Musk is not the only thrillionaire investing millions upon millions of dollars into the prospect of going to space, but he is definitely the most advanced of the group.

Much like his reading as a child, Musk absorbed everything he could about space and the technology needed to get there. Still, those already in the industry were skeptical of Musk's plans.

In June 2002, Musk created Space Exploration Technologies Corporation, or SpaceX. The company would not be working to create space stunts for publicity; its first goal was to make spacecraft for commercial travel. In other words, Musk wanted to send people into space for profit. He bought a warehouse in El Segundo, California, and created an office space that soon became filled with folding tables, Dell computers, and engineers working to design SpaceX rockets.

Much like Musk's other companies, SpaceX was a chance to change the way an existing industry did business. Musk thought SpaceX could modernize a high-tech industry he felt had not really changed since the Space Age of the 1950s and 1960s. A private space company could limit costs and fill a gap that the shrinking NASA was creating in the space industry.

Musk announced his first rocket would be called the

Falcon 1, a reference to the Millennium Falcon from the Star Wars films. He also announced a pay scale for moving certain amounts of weight to space with the Falcon 1.

SpaceX built an engine facility at its El Segundo warehouse, though the company later moved to Hawthorne, California. SpaceX also acquired a testing site in Texas. Engineers and scientists joined the company and worked with machinists to build custom engines and rocket parts.

The key to SpaceX's business model is to make reusable rockets. Most space mis-

Musk knew little about the aerospace industry when he started SpaceX, often quizzing the engineers and experts he hired so he could better understand the company's projects.

sions have huge costs because the rockets used to get things into space fall back to Earth and are destroyed. Musk wanted SpaceX's Falcon to eventually land itself back on Earth, reusing it to save money and limit the need to constantly make new rockets. "If one can figure out how to effectively reuse rockets just like airplanes, the cost of access to space will be reduced by as much as a factor of a hundred," Musk wrote on the

SpaceX website. "A fully reusable vehicle has never been done before. That really is the fundamental breakthrough needed to revolutionize access to space."[45]

The Texas Cattle Haul

SpaceX engineers got to work and built engines for the Falcon 1, an initial rocket called Merlin and a second stage rocket engine called Kestrel. Once the engines were built, everything was loaded up in a U-Haul and taken from Los Angeles to McGregor, Texas. SpaceX called the trip the Texas Cattle Haul. In Texas, the engineers fired the engines and worked out problems. They built a bunker and set up cameras to watch the rocket so they could study the footage if something went wrong.

SpaceX made a lot of noise and created some smoke, but their neighbors in Texas did not seem to mind. The farm animals, however, provided a fun distraction for the SpaceX group. "Cows have this natural defense mechanism where they gather and start

Musk is shown here watching the launch of a Falcon 1 rocket.

Avoiding Vacations

While Elon Musk was getting into rockets, he was also fighting off an illness that nearly killed him. In 2000, Elon and Justine took a trip to Brazil and South Africa. On the trip, Elon came down with a severe case of malaria. He was hospitalized and lost a lot of weight. Friends said he looked like a skeleton, and many were concerned about his mental state.

Musk joked that between the malaria and his ousting as CEO of X.com on his honeymoon, he has reasons to avoid vacations. "That's my lesson for taking a vacation: vacation will kill you,"[1] he said.

Musk still avoids vacations because he believes bad things always happen to him when he stops working: "The first time I took a week off, the Orbital Sciences rocket exploded and Richard Branson's rocket exploded ... the second time I took a week off, my rocket exploded. The lesson here is don't take a week off."[2]

1. Quoted in Kia Makarechi, "5 Things Elon Musk Fears," *Vanity Fair*, May 14, 2015. www.vanityfair.com/news/2015/05/5-elon-musk-fears.

2. Quoted in Kim Lachance Shandrow, "An Emotional Elon Musk Admits He's Only 'Tried' Twice to Take Two Weeks Off in Past 12 Years," *Entrepreneur*, September 29, 2015. www.entrepreneur.com/article/251186.

running in a circle," said Jeremy Hollman, an early engineer at SpaceX. "Every time we fired an engine, the cows scattered and then got in that circle with the younger ones placed in the middle. We set up a cow cam to watch them."[46]

Musk would get daily calls from the crew in Texas about what went right and wrong with the engines. He would sometimes take part in the testing, working out solutions with engineers in soon-ruined fancy clothes.

As the rockets were built, SpaceX began working with the

Department of Defense. The company was contracted to launch a satellite called TacSat-1 using the Falcon 1. In December 2003, Musk and SpaceX showed a Falcon 1 prototype to the public. The company built a mockup of the 7-story high Falcon 1 and its mobile launch system and hauled it to Washington, D.C., to the Federal Aviation Administration's (FAA) headquarters. The event got a lot of attention, and a few weeks later, SpaceX announced a second rocket design: the Falcon 5.

First Problems

The Falcon 1's first flight was scheduled for 2004, but it was delayed. There were many problems that caused the delay. In May 2005, SpaceX finally moved its Falcon 1 rocket to the Vandenberg Air Force Base near Los Angeles for its first test— a 5-second engine burn. Vandenberg officials, however, were making it difficult for SpaceX to actually launch its Falcon 1 from the base. Lockheed Martin and other aerospace companies made it clear they were not happy about a newcomer using facilities nearby. Despite spending $7 million at Vandenberg, SpaceX was not allowed to use its Complex 3 West launch site to get the Falcon 1 into space.

"It's like you build your house … somebody else builds a house next to you and tells you to get out of your house,"[47] Musk told Space.com in 2005. Instead, SpaceX prepared a launch site on the island of Kwajalein, which was part of the Republic of the Marshall Islands. On March 24, 2006, the Falcon 1 was finally ready for launch. However, the launch was a failure. A fire started above the Merlin engine, and the Falcon 1 fell back to Earth and was destroyed. Musk was disappointed but not deterred.

"It is perhaps worth noting that those launch companies that succeeded also took their lumps along the way," Musk wrote after the crash. "SpaceX is in this for the long haul and … we are going to make this work."[48]

Deadlines and Dependability

One problem that plagued many of Musk's ventures was not hitting deadlines. Musk has often had to explain why his products failed to launch when first expected. For SpaceX, much of that is a simple problem of not understanding just how long it takes to get things right in the aerospace industry. "I think I just didn't know what … I was talking about," Musk said of the first deadline he set for SpaceX—a 2003 launch of the Falcon 1. "The only thing I had prior experience in was software, and, yeah, you can write a bunch of software and launch a website in a year. No problem. This isn't like software. It doesn't work that way with rockets."[49]

Critics have said that, even today, Musk still makes promises his companies cannot keep. Some say it is an unfair practice to keep making impossible deadlines for his company, raise hype for his products, and then inevitably push back his completion dates, leading investors on. However, Musk is steadfast in his belief that his goals—all of them—are achievable. He described his approach to deadlines at length to Vance:

> I certainly don't try to set impossible goals. I think impossible goals are demotivating. You don't want to tell people to go through a wall by banging their head against it. I don't ever set intentionally impossible goals. But I've certainly always been optimistic on time frames. I'm trying to recalibrate to be a little more realistic.

> I don't assume that it's just like 100 of me or something like that. I mean, in the case of the early SpaceX days, it would have been just the lack of understanding of what it takes to develop a rocket. In that case I was off by, say, 200 percent. I think future programs might be off by anywhere from like 25 to 50 percent as opposed to 200 percent.

So, I think generally you do want to have a timeline where, based on everything you know about, the schedule should be X, and you execute towards that, but with the understanding that there will be all sorts of things that you don't know about that you will encounter that will push the date beyond that. It doesn't mean that you shouldn't have tried to aim for that date from the beginning because aiming for something else would have been an arbitrary time increase.[50]

Frustrating Failure and Surprising Success

By 2006, Musk had invested more than $100 million of his own money into SpaceX. In March 2007, another Falcon 1 was launched. This time, the rocket did what it was

In 2008, NASA showed its confidence in SpaceX by contracting the company to make trips to the ISS.

supposed to do, its first and second engines firing correctly. After 5 minutes, though, the rocket began to wobble. The Falcon 1 then exploded. It was an improvement, but overall, it was another failure for the company. Still, Musk was committed to making SpaceX successful.

SpaceX's toughest year was 2008, which was when it nearly ran out of money. Despite the struggles, Musk rallied funding for his company and received a surprise at year's end when NASA awarded a $1.6 billion contract to SpaceX to run 12 flights to the ISS. SpaceX was back in business.

The Dragon Takes Off

On June 4, 2010, the Falcon 9 took flight. Named for the nine engines that power its first stage, it replaced the Falcon 5. SpaceX's Falcon 1 continued to have issues on launches. Musk worked tirelessly to avoid delays on further testing and launches, pushing for his employees to solve problems and streamline processes. SpaceX also began to market the launches better, hosting webcasts and creating hype for the

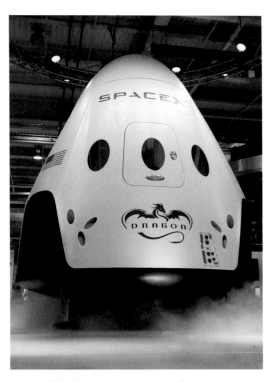

SpaceX's Dragon spacecraft was built to put humans into Earth's orbit, essentially replacing NASA's space shuttle program.

company's progress.

The 224.4-foot (68.4 m) tall, two-stage Falcon 9 became SpaceX's signature product. It delivered its shuttle capsule, the Dragon, to the ISS, in 2012. With that successful delivery, SpaceX became the first commercial company to ever reach the ISS.

The Dragon was SpaceX's newest project at the time. It was designed to carry cargo and humans into space. The Dragon project is an attempt to replace NASA's space shuttle program, which retired in 2011. SpaceX was awarded part of a contract to take astronauts to the International Space Station by 2017.

Landing on Earth

Part of Musk's ambitions with SpaceX in making reusable rockets involved them landing safely back on Earth. Falcon 9's third ISS resupply mission, which took place in 2014, featured a splashdown in the ocean. The goal was to slowly figure out a way to land a Falcon 9 on a solid surface. After an aborted first attempt, the first vertical landing of a Falcon 9 on a solid surface ended in a crash. The rocket, which was supposed to land on a floating barge in the ocean, landed too hard and crashed.

SpaceX attempted a number of landings, inching closer each time to achieving success. A Falcon 9 exploded after launch in June 2015, but in December of that year, a Falcon 9 was landed upright at Cape Canaveral, Florida. On April 8, 2016, SpaceX successfully landed a Falcon 9 upright on a drone ship in the ocean near Cape Canaveral on its fifth attempt.

The news has not been all good for the Falcon 9, though. On September 1, 2016, a Falcon 9 exploded on the launch pad during a test. The accident destroyed the rocket and a satellite SpaceX was launching that was going to be used by the social networking company Facebook. Each accident has been a significant setback for SpaceX, as it now has to meet client demands as well as expectations it has set for itself.

When the Falcon 9 rocket exploded in September 2016, SpaceX underwent a lengthy investigation to find out the cause of the accident. Although Musk had publicly suggested enemies of SpaceX may have had something to do with it, SpaceX announced in October that sabotage was not the likely cause of the explosion.

Musk, however, was still worried that sabotage could be the cause of a future explosion, and he wanted to work to protect against that possibility:

The Falcon 9 rocket is SpaceX's most iconic product, sending its Dragon to the ISS and landing upright in 2016.

We can exactly replicate what happened on the launch pad if someone shoots the rocket. We do not think that is likely this time around, but we are definitely going to have to take precautions against that in the future. We looked at who would want to blow up a SpaceX rocket. That turned out to be a long list. I think it is unlikely this time, but it is something we need to recognize as a real possibility in the future.[51]

People on Mars

In 2016, Musk and SpaceX officially unveiled their plan to colonize Mars. The moon, Musk said, is old news. "I'm less interested in the [m]oon," he told Space.com in 2005. "I think we saw that movie in the 1960s … it's a 60's re-run. A remake is never as good as the original."[52]

The plan, unsurprisingly, involves a gigantic rocket. The unnamed rocket is designed to be larger than the famous Saturn V that launched astronauts to the moon in NASA's Apollo space program. The Saturn V was 363 feet (111 m) tall, the height of a 36-story building. Musk's massive rocket is expected to be 400 feet (122 m) tall and about 39 feet (12 m) wide—about 6.5 feet (2 m) wider than the Saturn V. Decades later, the Saturn V rocket is still the most powerful ever launched, but Musk's would be 3.5 times more powerful.

The spacecraft would be filled with up to 100 people. Once in the air, it would detach from the rocket and use its own boosters to get past Earth's atmosphere. Then, it would orbit Earth, getting refueled by the giant rocket after the rocket landed back on Earth and was sent back into space. That massive rocket would then land itself back on Earth, be given a supply of fuel, and return to the ship in orbit again and again until the ship is ready to head toward Mars.

Using that fuel, the craft would need to blast itself to interplanetary speed, then coast for a few months to make the long journey. Then, SpaceX says, the craft will slow itself down using Mars's atmosphere and land itself, and the passengers would begin the colonization of Mars. The company hopes the craft will be reusable, which means it will come back to Earth after making its own fuel on Mars. Some experts have called that the hardest part of the plan, though the craft's engine would use cold liquid methane for fuel, which SpaceX thinks can be made on Mars.

The plan to get the first 100 people to Mars is part of a 4-step plan to colonize the Red Planet with 1 million people. The first step could happen as soon as 2018 according to SpaceX, with a

Musk has said only 5 percent of SpaceX is working on its mission to Mars, but he does expect the mission to be successful.

Dragon spaceship sent to Mars to conduct scouting missions. In 2016, SpaceX announced it would send a Red Dragon to Mars to "inform the overall Mars colonization architecture."[53] The second part of the plan would be to send a fuel factory to Mars to provide resources for missions and the eventual craft filled with people ready to colonize Mars. This step in the plan involves robots designed to search for water, solar energy, and forms of methane the colony could use to make fuel needed to sustain further research and launch rockets. The next step would be the manned spaceship.

"We want to establish a steady cadence—that there's always a flight leaving, like a train leaving the station," Musk said. "With every Mars rendezvous we will be sending a Dragon ... [and] at least two or three tons of useful payload to the surface of Mars."[54]

Chapter Five

Wheels
and Batteries

While Musk was dreaming of life on Mars, he had his feet—and wheels—firmly planted on the ground. An avid car enthusiast, Musk did not wait to sell his third company before investing in his next venture.

Tesla Motors was started in 2003 by Marc Tarpenning and Martin Eberhard, who wanted to make a car powered by a lithium-ion battery. The company was named after Nikola Tesla, an inventor who contributed greatly to the development of electricity supply systems. The group soon added Ian Wright and hired electric car expert JB Straubel. The group approached Musk to invest in the company, and he immediately took to their idea. Musk invested $6.5 million in the company, making him its largest shareholder. He was also named Tesla's chairman.

Though the Tesla team knew little about the automobile industry and was not even sure the technology they wanted to use could work, they solved that problem the same way Musk and many others in Silicon Valley solve such problems—hiring young, hungry engineers to throw themselves into creating solutions.

The company hired a stable of engineers and found a building in San Carlos, California, to get to work. Tesla Motors had a single toolbox when it first started working on its electric cars. The company's goal was to build Tesla's first car—the Tesla Roadster—to be delivered to customers by early 2006. Like all projects involving Musk, though, it took much longer than they anticipated. The company's first prototype, a black roadster called engineering prototype one (EP1), was ready in May 2006. A second prototype, the red EP2, was ready a couple of months later. Musk showed them both off in July of 2006.

The unveiling was a major event. Vance wrote, "Celebrities like then-governor Arnold Schwarzenegger and former Disney CEO Michael Eisner showed up at the event, and many of them took test rides in the Roadsters."[55] It seemed Tesla Motors was ready to make a big splash in the automobile industry.

The Roadster

The $90,000 Roadster went from 0 to 60 miles (97 km) per hour in under 4 seconds. Its top speed was more than 130 miles (209 km) per hour. A Tesla Roadster could go 250 miles (402 km) per charge on its battery. Other venture capitalists soon began investing in Tesla and were excited about is potential. Musk also continued to invest.

The first Tesla Roadster went on sale in 2008. Tesla sold more than 2,400 roadsters in 30 countries, selling the car directly to customers instead of using car dealerships like other car companies. The success of the Roadster allowed the company to work on more inexpensive models. It is a strategy many businesses use when first growing—sell a few expensive versions of a product and slowly make it cheaper and more widely available. The television and refrigerator were often cited as examples of this practice by company executives in the media.

Tesla was selling cars, but its costs were difficult to keep down. The company realized it cost about $200,000 to make each car they sold for less than $100,000. Tesla was losing money, and

The Tesla Roadster was a convertible, which made it an ideal car for the rich and famous in California, who flocked to see it unveiled in 2006.

another CEO was brought in to replace Eberhard and right the ship. That CEO, Michael Marks, helped eliminate some problems and set a plan for Tesla moving forward.

By 2008, Musk had taken over as CEO of the company, and it was reported that Tesla was going to have to lay off 25 percent of its workforce. The company needed to raise money quickly or face bankruptcy. In hindsight, as the company grew, it may have looked like Tesla was always going to find success. However, in 2008, things truly were dire. The family of Musk's girlfriend at the time, Talulah Riley, even offered to mortgage their own house to help the company stay afloat. A website started a "Tesla Death Watch" and wrote endlessly about the company's mistakes.

For a time, Musk thought he would have to choose one of his two companies—SpaceX or Tesla—to invest in and ensure its survival. "I could either pick SpaceX or Tesla or split the money I had left between them," Musk once said. "That was a tough decision. If I split the money, maybe both of them would die. If I gave the money to just one company, the probability of it surviving was greater, but then it would mean certain death for the other company. I debated that over and over."[56]

Righting the Ship

By the end of 2008, Musk was officially running out of money. Tesla was spending about $4 million a month and needed another major round of funding. Kimbal Musk, who had also lost money during this period, invested what he could in Tesla. Musk somehow raised $20 million, which was enough to keep the company afloat.

Elon was a tough boss at Tesla. He would fire employees in the marketing department who made typos, even in emails. He would demand public relations employees "fix" negative stories about the company. His reputation as a driven, sometimes overbearing boss was fair, but Musk's management at Tesla was working. The

Much like SpaceX, Tesla's engineers were tasked with designing new parts to solve problems that other companies would spend much more money on or not try fixing at all.

Charging Stations
and Powerwalls

Electric vehicles need a place to recharge, another challenge Tesla Motors has taken on since its inception. The company offers customers the ability to install charging units in their homes to recharge Tesla vehicles, and it has also installed supercharging stations throughout the United States. This means people can actually use their electric vehicles to travel long distances, even going cross-country just like a traditional gasoline-powered vehicle.

Unlike gas stations, which are found throughout the world, electric charging stations have taken time to expand. However, Musk is confident the system will grow as more owners join the market and demand increases in the number of stations. Tesla hopes to build more stations that charge vehicles faster, making electric vehicles operate more like traditional cars while saving costs for drivers.

In 2015, Tesla announced the Powerwall, a rechargeable lithium-ion battery station that is installed in a home or business. The powerful battery costs a few thousand dollars and can actually store energy, lowering energy costs for individuals, families, and businesses. As Tesla has joined with companies such as SolarCity to manufacture energy, Musk's dream of energy-efficient living grows closer to a reality.

company continued to attract attention and refine its products to lower costs. Things began looking up for the company, which meant it was time to look toward the future.

This 2013 photograph shows a Tesla employee working on a Model S assembly line.

Expanding the Lineup

With the company finally solvent and costs under control, Tesla started to work on its second vehicle—the Model S. The prototype was shown for the first time on March 26, 2009. A few months later, Tesla was given a loan from the U.S. Department of Energy. The company has needed infusions of cash multiple times, but in 2013, it was the first car company to repay loans from the U.S. government with $12 million in interest.

The Model S is a sedan that can drive for more than 300 miles (483 km) per charge, depending on certain factors. The sleek vehicle won *Motor Trend* magazine's 2013 Car of the Year award, a huge accomplishment for a company with just two vehicles in its stable. The success of the Model S and the Roadster attracted attention from other car companies. Daimler invested in the company, and Tesla formed a strategic partnership with Toyota shortly before its IPO in June 2010, which raised a little more than $226 million for the growing company.

Telsa Motors continued to grow as shares of the company went up. In 2010, Tesla bought a former auto factory in Fremont,

Tesla's slick marketing and impressive cars have made it a favorite of auto enthusiasts, even if many cannot afford to buy one.

California, to produce its Model S where Toyotas and General Motors cars were once made. In 2012, Tesla announced its first sport utility vehicle (SUV), the Model X. With a 289-mile (465.1 km) range between charges and seating for 7, the car helped Tesla reach a new customer base. It also featured "falcon-wing doors," which lifted up automatically to allow hands-free entry to the vehicle. It was a fancy perk on an SUV, but with the addition of the Model X, the company was becoming more than just a luxury car brand.

Musk once called the Model X "the most difficult car in the world to build."[57] Why did he push ahead on building it, even when he realized how difficult the process would be? He wanted to expand the market for Tesla, which would be further expanded with the addition of another model. "The Model X allows us to double our addressable market," Musk said in 2015. "The S and X serve as the revenue foundation for the Model 3."[58]

The Model 3—announced officially in 2015—was Tesla's most affordable vehicle yet. Tesla offered reservations to customers for

Safety Concerns

One aspect of Tesla's vehicles Musk takes pride in is their safety. Teslas routinely lead in crash-test safety categories. However, as Tesla has expanded its technological offerings, it has experienced tragedy. Tesla's controversial autopilot features on its cars came into the spotlight in 2016 when a man became the first to die in a Tesla vehicle accident. A Model S driver engaged Tesla's autopilot feature—which allowed for hands-free driving on highways—when the Model S crashed into a white tractor-trailer. Tesla released a statement about the accident and assured drivers its technology is safe, but it sparked a conversation about driverless technology in vehicles, which is something Tesla continues to implement as software advances are made in its cars.

$1,000. More than 370,000 customers signed up to reserve a Model 3 in 2016. Tesla is scheduled to finally deliver its first Model 3s to customers in 2017. Musk has hinted at further projects for Tesla Motors, including electric commercial vehicles.

Even though Tesla Motors continues to grow its client base and create new vehicles, its future is still tied to its current success. Musk has admitted that sales figures lead directly to the company's ability to make new models in the future and to continue producing the Model 3s in the present. "In order for us to produce the Model 3, we are critically dependent on the revenue we receive from the people that buy the Model S and Model X," Musk said in 2016, "So, it's important to bear in mind … the thing that is enabling the Model 3 to exist, is fundamentally the people that are buying the Model S and Model X today and historically."[59] Musk has said that the more expensive cars will always have the more advanced technology because that technology has to trickle down to the Model 3 to keep it relatively affordable.

Musk's interest in science and bettering humanity may take him in wilder directions in the future.

Saving Life on Earth

Musk's philosophy for how he goes about his life and his work was established early on and was greatly impacted by science fiction. He truly believes that for human life to exist moving forward—not just a few years or decades in the future, but centuries and millennia from now—people needed to further explore the solar system to find new places for humans to live. He understands the science behind climate change that says human activity may have ruined life on Earth for the long term. For Musk, this means alternatives to living on Earth must be found. This is why he is focused on making life sustainable not—as many have imagined before him—on the moon, but on Mars.

Though Tesla Motors works to reduce carbon emissions in its vehicles and strives for environmental responsibility, Musk has said he is not an extremely environmentally conscious person or businessman. "I'm not really super hardcore about being ultra environmental in all things," Musk told *Forbes* magazine's Hannah Elliott in 2002. "Because I think you don't want to make life miserable. We want to create a better future, but a better future is not one where we are constantly depriving ourselves of the things we love."[60]

Elliott asked about Tesla's commitment to using renewable resources to power its cars, while Musk's SpaceX still relies on refined jet fuels to power its rockets and explore space. Musk said that, while he does think renewable resources can be used to power rockets eventually, research and exploration should not be limited just because the current technology to do so using renewable resources does not yet exist:

> The reason I wanted to create the Roadster was to show that you could have an electric car that's better than a gasoline car. Ultimately, I believe we can create a rocket that uses renewable fuels—a fuel that's actually created from sunlight and electricity … that uses electricity, water, and carbon dioxide—but until we do, we must still have [fuel-powered] rockets. And so we need to figure out how to have the things we love and not destroy the world. That's the trick of it.[61]

As SpaceX's technology improves, its rockets may become more environmentally responsible in the same way Tesla's cars are more environmentally responsible than gas-powered cars. However, for now, Musk believes he needs to pollute Earth a bit more with rocket fuel to save humanity.

Chapter Six

Solar Panels, Tunnels, and Beyond

Musk still serves as CEO of both Tesla Motors and SpaceX, but he has also expanded his interests to other projects. Some of these are related to his current holdings and have even become part of his existing companies. Others are simply related to things Musk is fascinated by—transportation, sustainability, and helping humankind survive well after he is gone.

The Hyperloop

In 2013, Musk had an idea about changing a system of transportation that had nothing to do with space travel or futuristic cars. On SpaceX's website, he proposed what he called "the Hyperloop." The idea started with the announcement of high-speed rail for California, a state filled with infrastructure and traffic issues that seem by some to be impossible to fix. On the SpaceX website, Musk wrote,

> When the California "high speed" rail was approved, I was quite disappointed, as I know many others were too. How could it be that the home of Silicon Valley and JPL [NASA's Jet

Musk on the Big and Small Screens

Musk is often seen in news stories or on panels talking about his various businesses and technological plans. However, he can also be seen in movies and on television shows. Perhaps his most famous film appearance is his brief cameo in *Iron Man 2*, but he has also appeared in the 2016 film *Why Him?*, the 2013 film *Machete Kills*, and the 2005 film *Thank You for Smoking*, which he also contributed to as an executive producer.

Musk has also been featured on television shows, including an episode of *The Big Bang Theory*. He has lent his voice to episodes of both *South Park* and *The Simpsons*, and he has appeared on various talk shows, such as *The Late Show with Stephen Colbert* and *Late Night with Jimmy Fallon*. Musk's comfort in front of the camera has helped create the image of him as a real-life Tony Stark.

Propulsion Laboratory]—doing incredible things like indexing all the world's knowledge and putting rovers on Mars—would build a bullet train that is both one of the most expensive per mile and one of the slowest in the world? Note, I am hedging my statement slightly by saying "one of." The head of the California high speed rail project called me to complain that it wasn't the very slowest bullet train nor the very most expensive per mile.

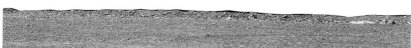

Musk believes the Hyperloop will become a reality.

The underlying motive for a statewide mass transit system is a good one. It would be great to have an alternative to flying or driving, but obviously only if it is actually better than flying or driving. The train in question would be both slower, more expensive to operate (if unsubsidized) and less safe by two orders of magnitude than flying, so why would anyone use it?[62]

Musk argued that a new transportation system should be built—one that is safer, faster, more convenient, and cheaper than high-speed rail or even car travel. Musk's other requirements were for it be immune to weather, self-powered, and resistant to earthquakes.

Musk released to the public a 58-page paper about Hyperloop Alpha, his plan for a high-speed transportation service that uses pod-like vehicles to move goods and people through an enclosed tube at high speeds. A tube system would be built for the pods to travel in. Basically, the pods would move in a vacuum, getting sucked through the tube at a top speed of

760 miles (1,223.1 km) per hour.

The Hyperloop has been described as "completely impractical"[63] by some experts, but the project received immense media attention when Musk first wrote about it. Some companies even began working to build test pods to see if this idea could become a reality. SpaceX announced a weekend for these companies to test their human-scale pods at a track they built on their Hawthorne campus in early 2017. Through what has been named the Hyperloop Pod Competition, SpaceX hopes these companies can produce working pods that can help further refine the idea into a real form of transportation in the future.

The Rives and SolarCity

Elon Musk's cousins Peter and Lyndon Rive also became entrepreneurs. In 2006, with the help of Musk, they started a company called SolarCity. The company makes and installs solar panels on commercial homes and businesses. The panels collect energy from the sun. This reduces utility bills for people who typically get their power from the electrical grid. SolarCity also began creating vehicle charging stations, which electric vehicles such as Teslas need at certain points around the country to recharge quickly.

This mutual interest in the sustainable energy industry was no accident—Musk invested in SolarCity and worked closely with his cousins to grow the company. He still serves as its chairman.

As Tesla and SolarCity grew closer, the solar company continued to introduce new products. In 2016, it debuted a new type of solar panel that did not just go on top of the roof of a home or business but actually protected the home by serving as the roof itself. This technology fixes a main complaint of solar energy—that it sits on top of a roof and looks strange, even ugly—and expands the market to people looking to replace their roof.

SolarCity panels such as these can be found on homes and businesses.

"I think this is really a fundamental part of achieving differentiated product strategy, where you have a beautiful roof," Musk said in August 2016. "It's not a thing on the roof. It is the roof."[64]

These solar, or photovoltaic (PV), energy-generating devices were an exciting development the company hopes will bring more people into the growing market. Asphalt roofs are most common in the United States, but they absorb a lot of heat and do nothing with the energy they absorb. Eventually, they need to be replaced because of weathering and wear. SolarCity's new product is an easy way to replace a roof, lower utility costs, and have a beautiful home.

"If your roof is about to need to be replaced, you don't want to invest in solar panels to install on it since you are about to take it down," Lyndon Rive said in 2016. "But if the solar panels are the roof and you need to redo it anyway, there's no reason not to go with a power-generating roof."[65]

Musk and his cousins believe in solar panel technology and its viability as a business, but making it financially successful means convincing people not only that solar technology works, but also that it is cheap and easy to adopt. "If they come out with a solar panel that's 2 percent more efficient than the existing one, it won't move the needle," Lyndon Rive told *Newsweek* in 2009. "You have to make it easier for people to adopt the technology."[66]

Joining Forces for a Sustainable Future

In August 2016, Tesla Motors and SolarCity announced in a joint statement that Musk bought the solar power company for $2.6 billion. The acquisition was part of Musk's second master product plan for Tesla, which expanded the company's future strategy toward the creation of commercial buses, trucks, and ride-sharing programs that could even drive themselves. The development of solar roofs was another part of this plan.

The goal of all of this, of course, is to use new technology and sources of energy to save the planet. When unveiling his second master product plan in 2016, Musk said, "We must at some point achieve a sustainable energy economy or we will run out of fossil fuels to burn and civilization will collapse … The faster we achieve sustainability, the better."[67]

Musk said Tesla and SolarCity should have been combined long ago. "It is really an accident of history that the companies are even separate,"[68] he told CNBC after announcing the merger.

Musk said the merger would save him $150 million in 2017 alone, and it would give Tesla an edge in getting energy-efficient, low-cost power options to more customers around the world:

Musk Gets Political

The period surrounding the 2016 U.S. presidential election was a divisive time for America, including within the tech industry. Though many supported Democratic Party nominee Hillary Clinton, businessman Donald Trump was elected president. Musk said the election was not "the finest moment in [American] democracy in general." He also stated, "I feel a bit stronger that [Trump] is not the right guy ... He doesn't seem to have the sort of character that reflects well on the United States."[1]

Despite his critical comments, Musk, who became a U.S. citizen in 2002, later accepted a role as an adviser to Trump as part of his Strategic and Policy Forum, which was created to focus on the development and maintenance of strong American businesses.

1. Quoted in Robert Ferris, "Donald Trump's Character Reflects Poorly on United States, Elon Musk Says," CNBC.com, November 4, 2016. www.cnbc.com/2016/11/04/donald-trumps-character-reflects-poorly-on-united-states-says-elon-musk.html.

Musk can be seen in this photograph of a meeting between Donald Trump and leaders of the technology industry.

To solve the sustainable-energy question, we need sustainable-energy production, which is going to come primarily in the form of solar ... Combine that with stationary storage and an electric vehicle and you have a complete solution to a sustainable-energy future ... Those are three parts that are needed. And those are three things that I think Tesla should be providing.[69]

Some think the merger means that Musk will continue to work on his ultimate dream of building a solar-powered car, suggesting that the ingredients are there for it—the solar panels, the energy storage units, and the car manufacturing technology itself. Getting all three into one package in a car people will actually buy still seems like a far-off dream, but it continues to appear likely that Musk will attempt to build a solar-powered vehicle as technology improves.

Artificial Intelligence

As technology has advanced, many people, including many leading minds in the tech industry, have turned at least some of their attention toward artificial intelligence. This is the ability for a machine to perform tasks that previously required human intelligence and to simulate human behavior. Artificial intelligence, or AI as it is sometimes called, is considered controversial in some circles and has been the topic of science fiction films and television shows for decades.

Musk has been wary of artificial intelligence in the past, and he called it humanity's "biggest existential threat" during an interview at the Massachusetts Institute of Technology in October 2014. "With artificial intelligence we're summoning the demon,"[70] he said.

In 2015, Musk donated $10 million to the Future of Life Institute. The Institute is focused on finding ways to use artificial intelligence to benefit and not harm humans. As Musk said, "There is always some risk that in actually trying to advance AI we may create the thing we are concerned about."[71] Musk donated to the Institute because he believed in its mission of creating safe AI technology, which is in line with his general philosophy of doing whatever he can to preserve humanity.

By the end of 2015, however, Musk was no longer content to let another company handle research into safe AI technology. Instead, he and Sam Altman introduced their new company, OpenAI, in December of that year. Altman, the CEO of Y Combinator, which provides funding for tech start-ups, joined with Musk and others to create a nonprofit AI research company that wants to build safe AI that would be widely available to many different groups that would responsibly use it.

Many tech companies are so interested in developing AI that they tried to essentially stop the company from happening, offering large salaries to the engineers and researchers joining the project. Wojciech Zaremba, a researcher who joined OpenAI, described the situation to *Wired* magazine in 2016:

"The amount of money was borderline crazy … "

How many dollars is "borderline crazy"? Two years ago, as the market for the latest machine learning technology really started to heat up, Microsoft Research vice president Peter Lee said that the cost of a top AI researcher had eclipsed the cost of a top quarterback prospect in the National Football League—and he meant under regular circumstances, not when two of the most famous entrepreneurs in Silicon Valley were trying to poach your top talent. Zaremba says that as OpenAI was coming together, he was offered two or three times his market value.

OpenAI didn't match those offers. But it offered something else: the chance to explore research aimed solely at the future instead of products and quarterly earnings, and to eventually share most—if not all—of this research with anyone who wants it. That's right: Musk, Altman, and company aim to give away what may become the 21st century's most transformative technology— and give it away for free.

Zaremba says those borderline crazy offers actually turned him off—despite his enormous respect for companies like Google and Facebook. He felt like the money was at least as much of an effort to prevent the creation of OpenAI as a play to win his services,

The Giving Pledge

Elon Musk enjoys spending some of his billions on fancy cars, fast planes, and other luxuries. However, he is also known for his generosity. In fact, in 2012, Musk signed the Giving Pledge, which states that he plans to donate at least 50 percent of his wealth to charitable causes during his lifetime or upon his death. The Giving Pledge was started by billionaires Warren Buffett, Bill Gates, and Melinda Gates to inspire other wealthy members of society to engage in philanthropic efforts.

After signing the Giving Pledge, Musk said, "This is not a change in what I am doing ... It is publicizing what I am doing in hopes that others will follow through."[1] He had already established the Musk Foundation, which deals mainly with clean energy, health care for children, and science education. Musk believes he is making the world a better place through his companies and his foundation.

1. Quoted in Carl J. Loomis and Miguel Helft, "12 More Billionaires Sign on to Buffett/Gates Pledge," *Fortune*, July 17, 2014. fortune.com/2012/04/19/12-more-billionaires-sign-on-to-buffettgates-pledge/.

and it pushed him even further towards the startup's magnanimous mission. "I realized," Zaremba says, "that OpenAI was the best place to be."

That's the irony at the heart of this story: even as the world's biggest tech companies try to hold onto their researchers with the same fierceness that NFL teams try to hold onto their star quarterbacks, the researchers themselves just want to share. In the rarefied world of AI research, the brightest minds aren't driven by—or at least not only by—the next product cycle or profit margin. They want to make AI better, and making AI better doesn't happen when you keep your latest findings to yourself.[72]

In 2016, OpenAI released its first AI software, which was essentially a toolkit others can use to build their own AI systems. The company hopes its tools and research can be used by countless tech companies to build safe artificial intelligence that helps improve human lives on Earth and, perhaps someday, elsewhere in the solar system.

What Will He Think of Next?

With nearly 7 million followers on the social networking platform Twitter, Elon Musk can create his own news with just a few words. Musk routinely updates people on SpaceX experiments and improvements to Tesla vehicles. He also writes about things he would like to do in the future. In December 2016, Musk tweeted about something millions of others tweet about daily without making the news: traffic woes. However, when a billionaire complains about traffic and proposes starting a new company to deal with it, journalists have to take his rants seriously.

Musk posted the following to Twitter on December 17: "Traffic is driving me nuts. Am going to build a tunnel boring

Could solving traffic problems by creating new tunnel systems be Musk's next project?

machine and just start digging…" In a few tweets that followed, Musk said the company would be called "The Boring Company." It would also have a slogan that says "boring, it's what we do." A few hours later, Musk tweeted "I am actually going to do this."[73] All four tweets got thousands of retweets and likes on the social media website as news of his tweets circled the globe many times over. Musk even changed his Twitter biography to reflect his apparent new ambition: "Tesla, SpaceX, Tunnels & Open AI."[74]

No one could tell if he was just kidding or if the billionaire actually wanted to start a tunnel boring company and invest in a new kind of transportation industry. That did not stop dozens of stories from being written about the series of tweets. Industry experts were even asked to predict what Musk might do next. If there is any true sign of the power of

What is Elon Musk going to do next? That question has led to much speculation and debate in the tech community.

Elon Musk, it is that those four tweets constitute real news.

The ideas of the boy who loved science fiction and comic books are not just childhood dreams anymore. Musk has taken much of his early ambition and turned it into real change. The boy from South Africa who used to be bullied for his unpopular passions and tendency to stare into space is now a major player in the global economy, and his interests can change entire industries forever.

Tunnels might be the future of Musk's international empire, or his plans could be a clever joke few understand. Either way, Musk is someone who must be taken seriously. His determination to change the world means that when he says he is going to do something, we should believe it.

Notes

Introduction: Comic Book Comparisons

1. Ashlee Vance, *Elon Musk: Tesla, SpaceX, and the Quest for a Fantastic Future*. New York, NY: HarperCollins, 2015, p. 17.

2. Quoted in Eric Johnson, "SpaceX CEO Elon Musk Has Done the 'Real' *Iron Man* Several Favors," *Recode*, October 12, 2016. www.recode.net/2016/10/12/13259344/elon-musk-iron-man-jon-favreau-tony-stark-spacex-recode-podcast.

3. Quoted in Xavier Harding, "Elon Musk Teases Iron Man Suit on Twitter," *Popular Science*, June 9, 2016. www.popsci.com/elon-musks-iron-man-suit.

4. Quoted in Vance, *Elon Musk*, p. 24.

Chapter One: South Africa to Canada

5. Quoted in Kerry A. Dolan, "How To Raise A Billionaire: An Interview With Elon Musk's Father, Errol Musk," *Forbes*, July 2, 2015. www.forbes.com/sites/kerryadolan/2015/07/02/how-to-raise-a-billionaire-an-interview-with-elon-musks-father-errol-musk/#16ad81077e1e.

6. Quoted in Vance, *Elon Musk*, p. 32.

7. Quoted in Vance, *Elon Musk*, p. 32.

8. Quoted in Vance, *Elon Musk,* p. 37.

9. Quoted in Vance, *Elon Musk,* p. 24.

10. Quoted in Vance, *Elon Musk,* pp. 38–39.

11. Quoted in Vance, *Elon Musk,* pp. 23–24.

12. Sean O'Kane "Play the PC Game Elon Musk Wrote as a Pre-Teen," *The Verge,* June 9, 2015. www.theverge.com/2015/6/9/8752333/elon-musk-blastar-pc-game https://blastar-1984.appspot.com/.

13. Quoted in Vance, *Elon Musk,* p. 46.

Chapter Two: Start-Ups and Sales

14. Quoted in Vance, *Elon Musk,* p. 59.

15. Quoted in Vance, *Elon Musk,* p. 60.

16. "History of Zip2, *Elon Musk,* SpaceX," eCorner, October 8, 2003. ecorner.stanford.edu/videos/397/History-of-Zip2.

17. "History of Zip2, *Elon Musk,* SpaceX."

18. "History of Zip2, *Elon Musk,* SpaceX."

19. "History of Zip2, *Elon Musk,* SpaceX."

20. "Driving With Elon Musk," YouTube video, 5:56, posted by *Forbes,* March 27, 2012. www.youtube.com/watch?v=R8PEnK3aoFQ.

21. "Driving With Elon Musk," YouTube video, posted by *Forbes.*

22. Quoted in Vance, *Elon Musk,* p. 68.

23. Quoted in Charles Cooper, "CitySearch, Zip2 to Merge in $300 Million Deal," ZDNet, April 3, 1998. www.zdnet.com/article/citysearch-zip2-to-merge-in-300-million-deal/.

24. Quoted in Vance, *Elon Musk,* p. 72.

25. Quoted in Vance, *Elon Musk,* p. 73.

Chapter Three: X Marks the Money

26. "LOST: Elon Musk, Before Paypal," YouTube video, 4:29, posted by The App Store Chronicle, September 23, 2014. www.youtube.com/watch?v=ZHKT3yxYvDQ.

27. Quoted in Vance, *Elon Musk,* p. 77.

28. Quoted in Vance, *Elon Musk,* p. 77.

29. Quoted in Jeffrey M. O'Brien, "The PayPal Mafia," *Fortune*, November 13, 2007. fortune.com/2007/11/13/paypal-mafia/.

30. Quoted in O'Brien, "The PayPal Mafia."

31. Quoted in Greg Sandoval, "X.com Chief to Step Down," CNET, January 2, 2002. www.cnet.com/news/x-com-chief-to-step-down/.

32. Quoted in Sandoval, "X.com Chief to Step Down."

33. Vance, *Elon Musk,* p. 89.

34. Justine Musk, "I Was a Starter Wife': Inside America's Messiest Divorce," *Marie Claire*, September 10, 2010. www.marieclaire.com/

sex-love/advice/a5380/millionaire-starter-wife/.

35. Musk, "'I Was a Starter Wife.'"

36. Quoted in Vance, *Elon Musk,* p. 117.

37. Musk, "'I Was a Starter Wife.'"

38. DEALBOOK, "Elon Musk, of PayPal and Tesla Fame, Is Broke," *New York Times*, June 22, 2010. dealbook.nytimes.com/2010/06/22/sorkin-elon-musk-of-paypal-and-tesla-fame-is-broke/?_r=0.

39. Elon Musk, "Elon Musk: Correcting The Record About My Divorce," *Business Insider*, July 8, 2010. www.businessinsider.com/correcting-the-record-about-my-divorce-2010-7.

40. Quoted in Lindsay Kimble, "Elon Musk's Ex Says They Could Get Back Together—After He's Spotted with Amber Heard," *People*, August 1, 2016. people.com/celebrity/elon-musks-ex-talulah-riley-on-reconciliation-following-amber-heard-sighting/.

41. Quoted in Vance, *Elon Musk,* p. 18.

Chapter Four: Rockets to the Stars

42. Quoted in Vance, *Elon Musk,* p. 98.

43. Quoted in Vance, *Elon Musk,* p. 101.

44. Quoted in Vance, *Elon Musk,* p. 100.

45. Quoted in "Reusability: The Key To Making Human Life Multi-Planetary," SpaceX, June 10, 2015. www.spacex.com/news/2013/03/31/reusability-key-

making-human-life-multi-planetary.

46. Quoted in Vance, *Elon Musk,* p. 124.

47. Quoted in Leonard David, "SpaceX Private Rocket Shifts to Island Launch," Space.com, August 12, 2005. www.space.com/1422-spacex-private-rocket-shifts-island-launch.html.

48. Quoted in Vance, *Elon Musk,* p. 140.

49. Quoted in Vance, *Elon Musk,* p. 231.

50. Quoted in Vance, *Elon Musk,* pp. 231–232.

51. Quoted in Peter B. de Selding, "SpaceX's Musk Says Sabotage Unlikely Cause of Sept. 1 Explosion, but Still a Worry," SpaceNews, October 17, 2016. spacenews.com/spacexs-musk-says-sabotage-unlikely-cause-of-sept-1-explosion-but-still-a-worry/.

52. Quoted in Davis, "SpaceX Private Rocket Shifts to Island Launch."

53. Quoted in Dave Mosher, "Elon Musk Just Shared His Ambitious 4-Step Plan for Colonizing Mars with a Million People," *Business Insider*, October 25, 2016. www.businessinsider.com/elon-musk-mars-colony-details-reddit-2016-10.

54. Quoted in Mosher, "Elon Musk Just Shared His Ambitious 4-Step Plan for Colonizing Mars with a Million People."

Chapter Five: Wheels and Batteries

55. Quoted in Vance, *Elon Musk,* p. 161.

56. Quoted in Vance, *Elon Musk,* p. 206.

57. Quoted in Benjamin Zhang, "Elon Musk: The Model X Is so Advanced We Probably Shouldn't Have Built It," *Business Insider*, October 3, 2015. www.businessinsider.com/elon-musk-the-model-x-is-so-advanced-we-probably-shouldnt-have-built-it-2015-9.

58. Quoted in Zhang, "Elon Musk: The Model X Is so Advanced We Probably Shouldn't Have Built It."

59. Quoted in Brooks Crothers, "Elon Musk Owns Tesla Model X Mistakes And Explains Migration of Model 3 Technology," *Forbes*, June 1, 2016. www.forbes.com/sites/brookecrothers/2016/06/01/elon-musk-candidly-details-tesla-model-x-issues-and-explains-migration-of-model-3-technology/#2ca6fc9128ba.

60. "Driving With Elon Musk," YouTube video, posted by *Forbes*.

61. "Driving With Elon Musk," YouTube video, posted by *Forbes*.

Chapter Six: Solar Panels, Tunnels, and Beyond

62. "Hyperloop," SpaceX, August 12, 2013. www.spacex.com/hyperloopalpha.

63. Quoted in Troy Wolverton, "Wolverton: Elon Musk's Hyperloop Hype Ignores Practical Problems," *The Mercury News*, August 13, 2013. www.mercurynews.com/2013/08/13/wolverton-elon-musks-hyperloop-hype-ignores-practical-problems/.

64. Quoted in Oliver Milman, "Elon Musk Leads Tesla Effort to Build House Roofs Entirely out of Solar Panels," *The Guardian*, August 19, 2016. www.theguardian.com/technology/2016/aug/19/elon-musk-tesla-solar-panel-roofs-solarcity.

65. Quoted in Milman, "Elon Musk Leads Tesla Effort to Build House Roofs Entirely out of Solar Panels."

66. Quoted in Daniel Gross, "Why Alternative Energy Needs Financial Engineering," *Newsweek*, April 9, 2009. www.newsweek.com/why-alternative-energy-needs-financial-engineering-77319.

67. Quoted in Russ Mitchell and Charles Fleming, "Tesla's Stock Falls after Elon Musk Reveals his 'Master Plan,'" *Los Angeles Times*, July 21, 2016. www.latimes.com/business/autos/la-fi-hy-musk-master-plan-20160714-snap-story.html.

68. Quoted in Robert Ferris, "Tesla-SolarCity Merger May Even Be a Little Late," CNBC.com, November 4, 2016. www.cnbc.com/2016/11/04/tesla-solarcity-merger-may-even-be-a-little-late.html.

69. Quoted in Tim Mullaney, "Tesla-SolarCity Deal: Little Can Stand in Elon Musk's Way When He Wants

Something," CNBC.com, November 21, 2016. www.cnbc.com/2016/11/21/musk-got-what-he-wanted-in-tesla-solarcity-deal--how-about-investors.html.

70. Quoted in John Markoff (the *New York Times*), "Silicon Valley Investors to Bankroll Artificial-Intelligence Center," *The Seattle Times*, December 13, 2015. www.seattletimes.com/business/technology/silicon-valley-investors-to-bankroll-artificial-intelligence-center/.

71. Quoted in Markoff (the *New York Times*), "Silicon Valley Investors to Bankroll Artificial-Intelligence Center."

72. Quoted in Cade Metz, "Inside OpenAI, Elon Musk's Wild Plan To Set Artificial Intelligence Free," *Wired*, April 27, 2016. www.wired.com/2016/04/openai-elon-musk-sam-altman-plan-to-set-artificial-intelligence-free/.

73. Quoted in Mahita Gajanan, "Elon Musk's Next Venture to Tackle Traffic is Totally Boring," *Fortune*, December 18, 2016. fortune.com/2016/12/18/elon-musk-traffic-boring/.

74. "Elon Musk," Twitter, accessed January 5, 2017. twitter.com/elonmusk.

Elon Musk Year by Year

1971

Elon Musk is born in South Africa on June 28.

1983

Musk creates the video game *Blastar* and later sells it to a computer magazine.

1988

Musk moves to Canada.

1989

Musk begins attending Queen's University in Ontario.

1992

Musk begins his studies at the University of Pennsylvania.

1995

Elon and Kimbal Musk create Global Link Information Network, which becomes Zip2.

1999

Compaq buys Zip2 for $307 million; Musk becomes a millionaire and starts X.com, his second company.

2000

X.com and Confinity merge; Musk marries his college sweetheart, Justine, who has their first child, but the baby dies at 10 weeks old from SIDS.

2002

Online auction site eBay purchases PayPal for $1.5 billion; Musk founds SpaceX and becomes a U.S. citizen.

2003

A Falcon 1 prototype is unveiled to the public by SpaceX.

2004

Musk invests in Tesla Motors and welcomes twin sons with Justine.

2006

Musk and his wife welcome triplets, Tesla Roadster prototypes are unveiled, and SolarCity is founded.

2008

The Tesla Roadster officially goes on sale, SpaceX is contracted by NASA to make deliveries to the ISS, and Elon and Justine divorce.

2009

The first Tesla Model S prototype is unveiled.

2010

Musk marries Talulah Riley; the Falcon 9 rocket is launched.

2012

Falcon 9 travels to the International Space Station, Tesla announces the Model X, and Musk signs the Giving Pledge.

2013

The Tesla Model S receives *Motor Trend*'s Car of the Year award, and Musk proposes the Hyperloop on the SpaceX website.

2015

A Falcon 9 launch ends in an explosion, but later that year, a successful upright landing takes place; Tesla announces the Powerwall and Model 3; Musk donates $10 million to the Future of Life Institute; and Musk cofounds OpenAI.

2016

An explosion during a Falcon 9 launch leads to a major investigation; Tesla Motors acquires SolarCity, a solar panel company; Musk and Riley divorce for the second time; Musk reveals plan to colonize Mars; OpenAI releases first AI software; and Musk hints at starting a tunnel project.

Index

Picture Credits

Cover Kevork Djansezian/Stringer/Getty Images News/Getty Images; pp. 7, 72 HECTOR GUERRERO/Stringer/AFP/Getty Images; p. 9 AF archive/Alamy Stock Photo; p. 12 Fernando Leon/Stringer/Getty Images Entertainment/Getty Images; p. 14 Cyrus McCrimmon/Contributor/Denver Post/Getty Images; p. 17 Mark Von Holden/AP Images for SolarCity; p. 19 Neilson Barnard/Staff/Getty Images Entertainment/Getty Images; p. 22 SINITAR/Shutterstock.com; p. 25 Max Whittaker/Stringer/Getty Images News/Getty Images; p. 28 Osugi/Shutterstock.com; p. 31 ROBYN BECK/Staff/AFP/Getty Images; p. 33 Heritage Images/Contributor/Hulton Archive/Getty Images; p. 35 Justin Sullivan/Staff/Getty Images News/Getty Images; p. 38 Alex Wong/ Staff/Getty Images News/Getty Images; p. 40 I AM NIKOM/ Shutterstock.com; p. 43 Ryan Miller/Contributor/Getty Images Entertainment/Getty Images; p. 48 Helga Esteb/Shutterstock.com; p. 53 Dan Tuffs/Contributor/Getty Images News/Getty Images; p. 54 Axel Koester/Contributor/Corbis Historical/Getty Images; p. 58 courtesy of NASA; p. 59 NASA/Dimitri Gerondidakis; p. 61 NASA/ Jim Grossmann; pp. 63, 67, 69, 78 Bloomberg/Contributor/ Bloomberg/Getty Images; p. 66 Glenn Koenig/Contributor/Los Angeles Times/Getty Images; p. 70 Joe Raedle/Staff/Getty Images News/Getty Images; p. 76 David Becker/Stringer/Getty Images News/Getty Images; p. 80 The Washington Post/Contributor/ The Washington Post/Getty Images; p. 85 Bart Everett/ Shutterstock.com; p. 86 JERRY LAMPEN/Staff/AFP/Getty Images.

About the Author

Ryan Nagelhout is an author and journalist who specializes in writing about sports. He has written hundreds of books, with topics that include baseball superstar David Ortiz, the Apollo 11 moon landing, and digital encryption and decryption. As a journalist, he has covered sports, reviewed restaurants, and written features about the arts. Ryan has a bachelor's degree in Communication Studies from Canisius College in Buffalo, New York, with a minor in Classics. He enjoys spending time with friends playing board games, bouldering, and hiking the Niagara Gorge in his hometown of Niagara Falls, New York.